CW00429321

# Open Fidelity
## An A-Z Guide

Anna Sharman

Purple Sofa Publications

# Open Fidelity - An A-Z Guide

First published 2006
by Purple Sofa Publications
PO Box 58110
London SW8 1RX

ISBN Information
Print: 0-9553870-0-0 (978-0-9553870-0-5)
E-book: 0-9553870-1-9 (978-0-9553870-1-2)

Set in ITC BradleyHand and Gill Sans

Design and layout by Michael Preston Typographic Design
cloudwalker_3@hotmail.com

Printed and bound by WP Digital
info@wpdigital.co.uk

## Acknowledgements and Dedication

My gratitude to everyone who has supported this project is enormous. Thanks to all my family and to my friends and lovers, past and present, particularly Andy, Linda, Chris, Clare, Geoff, Emily, Eudora, Fiona, Gary, Daphne, Leif, Paul, Zoyee, Vince and others who might not want to be named.

Thanks to the many Quakers who have shown support and interest, particularly in Streatham and Peckham local meetings, Young Friends General Meeting, Woodbrooke and Quaker Quest.

Thanks to attendees of BiCon, Bisexual Underground and London Bi Women; to subscribers to the uk-poly email list and readers of my blog; to the intrepid readers of the first version of this book; and to those who ordered copies before publication.

For their expert assistance, thanks to Rachel Smart, Suzy Greaves, Michael Preston, Louise Bolotin, Meg Barker, Emily Dubberley, Ben Pink Dandelion, Ian, Jo, Jenny R and Chris S.

Finally, heartfelt thanks to the people who have contributed the most important part of this book and all my future books on this subject: the people who have shared their experiences with me and allowed me to quote their words anonymously. The quotes in this book are theirs, but much more importantly, many of the ideas here have arisen from my conversations with them.

This book is dedicated to them.

# Contents

# Introduction

This book is a brief taster of Open Fidelity, the first in a series of books looking at the same ideas from different angles.

Open Fidelity is a more honest way of having loving relationships. Fidelity means partners trying to keep the promises they make and being honest with each other. Open means that partners are open to the possibility of each of them loving other people. So you don't have to be monogamous to be faithful. Open Fidelity can solve some of the problems of both monogamous and unfaithful relationships.

If you are open and faithful, there is a world of possibilities to try. You and your partner (or spouse) could have short flings or longer-term lovers as well as your committed partnership. You could try swinging, going to sex parties or meeting another couple. Or you could seek several long-term loving relationships – usually known as polyamory.

Open Fidelity means negotiating agreements about how open your relationship will be, and then keeping to those agreements or renegotiating them when they no longer work. Happy, honest, responsible non-monogamous relationships are possible.

Browse through the letters in this book, in whatever order you like, to find out more.

*...is for Affairs.*

Have you found out that your partner has had an affair with someone else behind your back? This discovery is painful. A big part of it can be that they have lied to you. You might fear that they will leave you for the other person. You might feel that they have betrayed their promise to you to be monogamous. There are many other reasons for being upset by a secret affair.

Or have you ever had a secret affair yourself? Did you wish there was a way to tell your partner without hurting them? But even if your partner didn't find out, it still hurt the relationship – it is impossible to lie without losing respect for the person you're lying to. Don't be fooled by those who argue that affairs only cause problems when the secret gets out.

One solution to all this hurt might be for everyone just to stay monogamous. Many people do manage this for long periods of time, but many others keep on being attracted to new people, or even falling in love with new people, throughout their lives. Although it is possible to be like this and still stay monogamous, that can put a lot of strain on your relationship. When temptation calls and there is no accepted way of being honest about it, I can see why secret affairs happen.

But I propose another way: be open and honest about your attractions, negotiate with your partner and you might find you can have other lovers in a responsible way. It's called Open Fidelity.

*A is also for Anxiety* – **see J for Jealousy**
*and for Attraction* – **see S for Sexuality**

# B

...is for Bisexuality.

Bisexuality means attraction to both men and women. Few bisexuals are equally attracted to both sexes. Many people who call themselves straight, gay or lesbian have had been attracted to both men and women at some point.

Say a bisexual person gets together with someone they want to commit to forever; if they were monogamous this would mean ruling out sexual relationships with the other sex forever. For some bisexuals, this is too much to ask.

Open Fidelity offers a way out of this: promise commitment to the person of your dreams, but negotiate with them and see if you can live with each of you having other relationships or short flings.

Some people with bisexual partners allow them to have other lovers of the same sex. Jealousy is less likely in this arrangement because your partner can see what you see in others that they can't provide.

B is also for Bedrooms – **see Z for Zzzzz**
and for Bondage – **see S for Sexuality**

# C

...is for Compersion.

Compersion is the opposite of jealousy: a feeling of joy when you see your partner loving someone else. It's a bit like being happy for a friend who has passed their exams.

Compersion is the ultimate conclusion of the idea of 'if you love somebody, set them free'. To someone who feels jealousy rather than compersion when their partner has another lover, this can seem incredible. But it does happen, and when it does, it can be wonderful.

If someone feels compersion for you, if they are truly happy to see you loving others, this can be the most liberating and joyful feeling in the world.

The word compersion was coined by the polyamory community. Polyamory means loving more than one person and usually involves having more than one committed relationship at a time. Open Fidelity is broader, including people with only one committed but open relationship.

Another word for compersion is frubbliness.

C is also for Conflict – see **N for Negotiation**
and for Children – see **K for Kids**

# D

*...is for Defending your lifestyle.*

Those who have been brought up in a traditional kind of environment might find it hard to accept Open Fidelity as a moral and ethical choice. Here are a few ideas to help you defend your lifestyle when challenged by someone who is being judgmental:

- Open Fidelity means fewer affairs and fewer cheating spouses.

- Open Fidelity is about honesty.

- Open Fidelity is about responsibility – everyone is responsible for how they act on their desires, for listening to others (especially their partner) and for negotiating honestly.

- Open Fidelity means more disapproval of those who cheat on their partners – because they have no excuse. Why have sex with someone behind your partner's back when they wouldn't mind you doing it with their knowledge?

- Open Fidelity means that the deepest desires of each person are respected and given a chance to be fulfilled – but without hurting other people.

D is also for Divorce – **see E for Ending relationships**
and for Dating – **see Y for Young, free and single**

*...is for Ending relationships.*

Open Fidelity means that if you fall for someone else when you are in a committed relationship, you don't need to split up. So your relationships might last longer.

But Open Fidelity relationships do end, for many of the same reasons that monogamous ones do – someone breaks the rules and the other can't easily forgive them; or conflicts arise that can't be resolved; or people simply grow apart.

A relationship that doesn't last forever isn't a failure; it's something that was good for a time but needs to end. Value the time you have shared, even if it is now over. In Open Fidelity, you don't have to load all your expectations onto one relationship, so if that relationship ends you aren't necessarily devastated.

What you can't do in Open Fidelity is use 'I've met someone else' as an excuse to end a relationship. If the relationship needs to end, it needs to end – do your partner the favour of giving them the real reasons why.

Sometimes Open Fidelity relationships can go on longer than they really should, because partners can't find an easy excuse to split. Watch out for this and be honest with yourself if it really is time to end the relationship.

*E is also for Equality* – **see L for Love**
*and for Ex-partners* – **see X for eXes**

# F

...is for Fidelity (or Faithfulness).

The main tenet of Open Fidelity is that faithfulness and monogamy aren't the same thing. A person is faithful if they are loyal and trustworthy – they do what they agreed to do.

Faithfulness to a partner means keeping to the agreements you have made together, and telling each other about any problems or any temptations to break the agreements. It is better to renegotiate an agreement than to break it.

A couple could agree, for instance, to consult each other in all big decisions; being unfaithful would then mean making a decision that affects your partner's life significantly without consulting them first.

For married people, faithfulness and monogamy are often taken to mean the same thing, but that is only because the marriage vows generally imply a promise to be monogamous.

F is also for Fathers – **see K for Kids**
and for Freedom – **see O for Openness**

# G

...is for God.

Some religious people will give you the impression that the only right kind of sexual relationship is a monogamous, heterosexual one. But if you are willing to look at the principles behind each religion, Open Fidelity could be acceptable.

For instance, Jesus said 'love your neighbour' and 'love your enemies' and preached forgiveness. Jesus condemned adultery, but adultery is not the same thing as consensual, honest non-monogamy. Having more than one partner, or being in an open relationship with the full knowledge and consent of everyone involved, isn't mentioned at all in the Bible, so no one can say that the Bible forbids this.

I believe God (or the spirit, or the universal energy, whatever terms you prefer) leads us all to become better, more loving, more honest people if we listen to our inner voices or our consciences. Open Fidelity is about being honest, loving and faithful, things that should be recommended by any religion.

G is also for Gay – **see Q for Queer relationships**
and for Green-eyed monster – **see J for Jealousy**

# H

...is for Honesty.

Honesty is one of the central tenets of Open Fidelity. Open relationships only work if partners are honest with each other about other people they are attracted to or having a sexual relationship with.

But honesty goes further than this. In order to build happy relationships and to be honest with your partners or lovers, you need to know yourself and be honest with yourself about what you really want.

It can be all too tempting to go along with a suggestion from someone you love (for example that they take another lover) when deep down you find it very hard. This almost always backfires, as your resentment can build up and burst out later, to the surprise of your partner, who thought you were happy with the situation.

Take time to work out your true feelings, so that you can express them clearly and honestly to your partner.

H is also for Homosexual – **see Q for Queer relationships** and for Honeymoon period – **see M for Monogamy**

**I**

*...is for Individuals.*

Open Fidelity is about valuing each person individually and giving each person the freedom to be themselves – including you.

No one should be defined by their relationship role(s) alone, be that father, wife, gay man or woman with multiple partners.

No one should have their individuality suppressed by another person, which means that each person in a loving relationship needs to be careful not to exert power over the other(s).

Opening up the possibility of having more than one partner can also free you to be more than the person you are with your original partner. You can express other sides to your personality with other lovers, share different interests with them, try new things with them.

Sometimes, when your relationships get really complicated, remember that you also need time to spend on your own, doing your own thing. It is important to make time for this when you need it and to allow time for all partners and lovers to do the same.

I is also for Infidelity – **see A for Affairs**
and for Integrity – **see H for Honesty**

# J

...is for Jealousy.

The power of jealousy can be reduced if you see it as the complex mixture of emotions that it is.

If you think you are feeling jealous, could it be that you are afraid of losing your partner to their other lover? Or that they don't love you any more? Or are you envious that they are having fun and you are being left out?

Look carefully at your feelings and work out what you are really afraid of – are your fears justified? If your fears can be allayed, the jealousy can disappear.

Some people don't feel jealousy at all, or even feel the opposite (see C for Compersion). Others used to feel it but don't any more. Others feel it now and again but being secure in their relationships they can ignore it or even get a thrill from it. And still others find it keeps plaguing them – it can be impossible to remove it completely.

One thing is for certain: in the long run, jealousy won't be solved by forcing your partner to be monogamous if they don't want to be.

J is also for Joy – see **C for Compersion**
and for Judgmental – see **D for Defending your lifestyle**

# K

...is for Kids.

A common reaction to Open Fidelity is 'it might work for some people, but you couldn't do it if you have children'. But if two parents stay together and find love elsewhere at the same time, isn't that still better for their children than the parents being unhappy or even splitting up?

Open Fidelity means more communication, and this can only help with communication about other issues in a family.

Be as honest as you can with your children about your relationship. If the situation is explained in a way they can understand, with lots of opportunity to ask questions, they may well take it in their stride.

Bear in mind that it's neither fair nor realistic to ask a child to keep a secret. Whatever you tell your children, be prepared for everyone else to know too.

More partners can mean more people to help with the childcare!

K is also for Kinks – **see S for Sexuality**
and for Keeping the rules – **see F for Fidelity**

# Quotes about Open Fidelity

For me, fidelity means openness and truthfulness and sharing our lives with each other, and not concealing our own selves from each other.
> Tom

A man can provide something to Kevin that I can't, so I'm not necessarily jealous because it's not a replacement for me.
> KerryAnn

When you have a child, you don't think you can't have another child because you couldn't love them when you already love this one. So what's the difference with partners?
> Jennie

I loved Sylvia - enough even to decline the offer of sex with someone at a party. I believed I was being honourable. Her reaction was unexpected - she thought I'd done something to encourage this woman. I wished I'd actually done the deed! So I decided not to mention the occasional coffee dates as it only seemed to stir up trouble.
> Russell

I found I could love both Julie and David. Loving the one didn't diminish my love for the other. The one was a deep and enduring love - the anchor of my existence. The other was a life-giving and all-demanding passion.
> Helen

Communication is quite difficult for me sometimes. Even though I completely trust Kevin and I know he's not going to judge me, I still have a hard time telling him how I feel.
> KerryAnn

When Sue has sex with someone else, I tend to get very fidgety, a bit angry or uncomfortable, and maybe have to go out for a walk. I don't feel it's anything which Sue needs to be concerned about. It's a consequence of the agreement that we have together and which I'm entirely happy with.
Tom

Steven was primary to me, Arthur was secondary. Both were vital. At home with Steven, I made bread. Out with Arthur, we ate zabaglione. Why force a choice between bread and zabaglione?
Jill

Malcolm and I were, as it turned out after a while, not terribly sexually compatible, so that when one or other of us has found someone who (on an occasional basis) fulfils a need, then that's marvellous.
Colin

There were times I wished I could have developed a relationship with a woman, but I didn't because I didn't want to hurt Tony and it felt safer to stay monogamous. At the same time, I was trying to balance that with not hurting myself in terms of not repressing my sexuality.
Alexandra

When Sally and I were considering getting married we discussed my sexual habits and agreed that we couldn't vow fidelity, so we spent ages working out our own vows.
Russell

This is a small sample of the many hours of recorded interviews I have had with people who practise Open Fidelity in a range of ways. All the names have been changed and the interviewees have given their permission to be quoted.

# L

...is for Love.

Open Fidelity gives love a chance to grow throughout your life, free to be expressed when it appears, even when you are already in a committed relationship.

Love is not a cake that has to be shared out between people, with less for each when there are more people. Loving one person doesn't reduce your love for other people. Parents find they can love all their children and their partner too.

Love implies equality between lovers – if you love your partner and want something (such as a second lover) for yourself, it is only fair to give the same opportunity to your partner.

It means not manipulating or trying to control your partner but giving them equal power in the relationship.

Bringing a new love into your life is rather like having a new baby, in fact – it will certainly change your life and that of your partner. But this doesn't stop people having babies.

Although love is infinite, time and energy aren't – see T for Time management.

L is also for Lying – see A for affairs and H for honesty
and for Lust – see S for Sexuality

# M

...is for Monogamy.

Open Fidelity doesn't mean you have to have more than one partner if you don't want to. You can still be monogamous.

Many people tend to be attracted to only one person at a time and also get jealous easily – we could call them naturally monogamous people. But some people only want one partner while not experiencing much jealousy themselves, and others get jealous even while wanting more than one partner themselves. The two aspects of being naturally monogamous (a tendency towards jealousy and only wanting one partner) don't always go together.

Monogamous relationships are great for people who want them, such as naturally monogamous people of one or both these kinds. Monogamy can also be good even for those who would sometimes prefer more open relationships.

Monogamy can be a good idea when you are in the first phases of being in love (the 'honeymoon period', also called 'new relationship energy'), or when your relationship is going through a difficult patch.

Open Fidelity gives you more options. If you choose monogamy, you will at least be doing so knowing about the alternatives.

M is also for Marriage – see **W for Weddings**
and for Mr Right – see **O for Openness**

# N

*...is for Negotiation.*

One of the key principles of Open Fidelity is keeping the promises you make, and renegotiating them rather than breaking them if they start to seem difficult.

One aspect of this is avoiding making promises that you don't think you will be able to keep. Another aspect is agreeing rules with your partner, rather than just assuming you will keep to certain rules (such as being monogamous). So Open Fidelity needs a lot of negotiation.

Negotiation means communicating what your needs and wishes are, listening carefully to what your partner and others involved say and working out between you what the best way forward is. It also means being clear with yourself what you really need and what is just an extra that would be nice.

Negotiation can help to reduce jealousy. For example, your partner might get more jealous when you meet your lover in a particular restaurant, one that you and your partner often visit together. You could agree to meet the lover somewhere else instead.

N is also for Networks of relationships — see **V for Vees**
and for New relationship energy — see **M for Monogamy**

*...is for Openness.*

What does the 'open' in Open Fidelity mean?

It means accepting the possibility that each person can be attracted to more than one other person. What you do about that possibility depends on what you negotiate.

Some couples stay monogamous but tell each other about people they fancy; some allow each other one-night stands with other people but not ongoing lovers; others allow ongoing lovers as long as they have a chance to get to know them; and there are many other possible arrangements.

Another aspect of openness is the idea that finding the love of your life doesn't mean they will be everything you need, forever. They may be your perfect partner, for a long time or for life, but it is worth being open to the possibility that you might have interests they don't share, or sexual desires that they can't fulfil, or that someone else might enter your fantasies in the future.

Why not agree with each other that neither of you can fulfil all the needs of the other? You are then both freed up to get some of your needs fulfilled elsewhere without feeling guilty (as long as you are open about it).

*O is also for Out* – **see P for going Public**
*and for Over* – **see E for Ending relationships**

# P

*...is for going Public.*

At the moment, many people who practise Open Fidelity keep quiet about it. It can be even harder to 'come out' about being non-monogamous (which people see as a choice) than about being gay, lesbian or bisexual (because you can't choose your sexuality). Also, there is often the assumption that you are cheating on your partner.

Part of my philosophy is that coming out is a very important part of being fully human. Coming out as whatever you are, showing the world (or at least the people closest to you) what your sexuality is and what is most important to you in life, means you can be yourself wherever you go.

Coming out isn't just about whether you are gay, straight or bisexual but can encompass other things, including the kinds of relationships you have. Going public about your complex relationships is a way of integrating your love life into the rest of your life, so you can be a whole, happy human being.

Coming out also helps others who are practising Open Fidelity. The more people stand up and say 'I have an open relationship', the easier it will be for society in general to accept Open Fidelity, and the easier it will be for others to come out.

*P is also for Polyamory* – see **C for Compersion**
*and for Promises* – see **N for Negotiation**

...is for Queer relationships.

Just about all the ideas in this book apply to same-sex and opposite-sex relationships equally.

Gay men have been having open relationships since time immemorial. It seems to me that gay men are usually less worried than straight people about their partners having other lovers.

Lesbians have also had a tradition of non-monogamy: the radical feminists of the 1960s and 1970s said that all patriarchal structures like marriage and monogamy should be rejected.

For these reasons, if you're in a same-sex open relationship, you may find more acceptance of your non-monogamy in the queer community than in wider society. The bisexual community in particular is very accepting of responsible non-monogamy.

Gay men and lesbians are the pioneers in this field, and I have learnt a lot from them. The gay rights movement has won many of the battles that pave the way for acceptance of Open Fidelity in society. In the UK, it is now illegal in most situations to discriminate on the grounds of sexuality; this breakthrough will help to reduce discrimination against those with more than one partner.

Q is also for Quads – see V for Vees
and for Quotes – see pages 18 - 19

*...is for Rings.*

Wedding rings can be a very useful way of telling the world you are unavailable and that you are committed to someone. But if you practise Open Fidelity, you might still be available when you are in a committed relationship.

Here's a suggestion for a new system involving two kinds of rings. One ring would be a gold one that means 'I'm unavailable for a new sexual relationship' but doesn't say anything about whether you have a partner. This could be worn if you are either married or in a monogamous partnership but also if you are celibate or not wanting sex with anyone for now.

The other ring could be silver and would mean 'I'm committed to someone', whether or not you are available. This could be worn by people in either non-monogamous or monogamous committed relationships as a sign of their love.

Both rings would mean you are monogamous and taken, and no ring would mean you are free and single.

*R is also for Repression* – see S for Sexuality
*and for Responsibility* – see D for Defending your lifestyle

# S

...is for Sexuality.

Sexuality means whatever turns you on – there is no need to restrict the word to just mean attraction to people of the same or opposite sex.

Open Fidelity is a way of allowing everyone to work out their own true sexuality and to find ways of expressing it in a positive way, even if parts of that sexuality aren't compatible with the person they want to be with most of the time.

I have talked to a number of people who get turned on by things that could be considered kinky, such as being tied up (bondage), acting a dominant or submissive role, or dressing up in rubber or leather. These kinds of kinks or fetishes are very common but aren't widely acknowledged to be common. And others are attracted to men and women, or different types of men or women.

If your sexuality doesn't quite fit with your partner's needs, talk about this with each other and try to understand how you each feel. Maybe another lover might help to fulfil your needs.

S is also for Secondary partners – **see V for Vees**
and for Swinging – **see V for Vees**

# T

*...is for Time management.*

If you ask someone with several ongoing partners what the most difficult thing is about their situation, they usually talk about time management.

Although love may be infinitely expandable, time isn't. It can be a challenge to negotiate when to spend time with different lovers without making any of them feel left out – and without interfering with the time they spend with their other lovers.

If you're considering having more than one serious relationship, don't underestimate the time you will need to give to each person. Some people with several partners talk about relationships being their hobby – they don't have time for anything else!

You might need to have a regular schedule for each couple to spend time alone together, plus other times for three or four to be together and family times if there are children as well. For example, I know one triad, let's call them A, B and C; for them, Tuesdays are always for A and B to spend time together, Wednesdays for B and C and Thursdays for A and C, and the weekends are spent with all three together.

It is easier if you only have one primary partner and your other relationships are secondary or short term. In this case, it is important to put your primary relationship first and not let time with your lovers detract from time with your partner.

T *is also for* Triads – **see V for Vees**
*and for* Telling people – **see P for going Public**

...is for Utopia.


Imagine a world where Open Fidelity is a widely accepted option alongside monogamy. There would be less repression of people's sexuality, fewer unhappy relationships, and more people who were happy with the relationships they had found.

I think this might lead to a decrease in sexual violence, although this happens for complex reasons and Open Fidelity might be only part of the answer. People who had previously had no outlet for their sexual feelings would find it easier to get a lover (or lovers) who could relate to them, so they wouldn't be as likely to express these feelings destructively.

Marriages between three or more people would be common, and divorce would be a more positive process, with former partners regretfully marking the end of their commitment but celebrating the good times they have had together.

Tabloids would take no notice of celebrities with two or more partners, but they would treat as a scandal anyone who cheats, that is, who breaks the rules of their relationship.

One question remains: in this ideal world would the soaps and celebrity gossip mags have enough scandal to keep them going? In fact there would be lots of exciting stories. How about 'My two lovers don't get on', or 'I only said he could have a one-night stand and now his lover's moved in'?

U is also for Unfaithfulness – **see A for Affairs**
and for Unavailable – **see R for Rings**

# V

*...is for Vees, triads and other complicated diagrams.*

If you have two or more long-term partners, the relationships between them can get complicated. Polyamorous people have developed new words to describe their relationships.

One word is 'Vee', which means a three-way relationship in which one person has two partners who aren't partners with each other. Variations on this are 'Z' or 'W' relationships, in which four or five people are linked in a line.

If three people are all partners with each other, this is usually called a triad (I have also heard the terms 'trupple', 'thrupple' and 'couple-three'). A quad is where four people are all mutual partners.

Some people have a 'primary partner' and a 'secondary partner(s)'. Others have just one partner and only short flings with lovers or 'swinging' arrangements with other couples.

It can be fun to draw diagrams linking people with their partners, lovers, exes and *their* partners, lovers and exes – the diagram can start to look like knots!

V *is also for* Violence – see **U for Utopia**
*and for* Vows – see **F for Fidelity** and **W for Weddings**

# W

...is for Weddings.

If you practise Open Fidelity, you may want to make a public commitment to your partner and gain the rights and responsibilities that a legal marriage or civil partnership brings. But you may also have difficulty with the traditional assumption that marriage means monogamy.

It is possible to get round this by stating in the ceremony what you mean by faithfulness. Or you could have a commitment ceremony that isn't legally binding, instead of getting legally married, so that you can choose your own vows (although this means you lose the legal benefits). The civil partnership ceremony for same-sex couples in the UK (and several other countries) doesn't include any statement about faithfulness.

Three-way weddings aren't yet possible anywhere that I know of, although three people in the Netherlands registered themselves in a 'cohabitation contract' in 2005.

If marriage didn't have to mean promising monogamy for the rest of your life, more couples might get married and their relationships might be more stable and long-lasting as a result.

W is also for Wedding rings – see R for Rings
and for Women – see Q for Queer and B for Bisexuality

# X

...is for exes.

One of the clearest conclusions that has come out of my research on Open Fidelity is something I didn't expect. I found that people who practice honest non-monogamy are far more likely than other people to be friends with their ex-partners.

In hindsight, this makes total sense. In monogamous relationships, a new partner can see ex-partners as a threat, so people feel they have to hate their exes in order to 'move on' and meet someone new. Whereas if a new relationship is an open one, the new partner may be happy to be friends with an ex-partner, knowing that if there is some residual attraction, it isn't a threat to the new relationship.

Open relationships also allow deeper friendships. This is because there isn't that continual worry that you might be being too friendly to your married friend and that their spouse might feel threatened by your closeness.

Open Fidelity allows the boundaries to be set where they need to be, not where society dictates they should be.

X is also for exhilaration – see **C for Compersion**

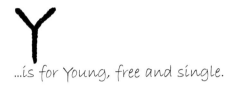

# Y

...is for Young, free and single.

Open Fidelity is all very well for those already in long-term relationships, you might be saying, but what if you're single?

Open Fidelity makes things more complex. How do you find a partner who wants the same kind of non-monogamous or monogamous relationship as you do?

The first answer is this: it is surprising how many people will consider the idea of Open Fidelity once it is explained fully. So be upfront when you meet someone you are attracted to, and tell them (at an appropriate time) what kind of relationship you are looking for.

Don't be put off if the person you are interested in is already in a committed relationship: Open Fidelity means that they could be open to another relationship. But it will take some talking to find out whether their arrangement is compatible with what you want.

There are now quite a few internet dating sites that ask lots of questions about relationship styles, so they can match up people who are into the same things.

Y is also for You — see I for **Individuals**
and for Yes to Open Fidelity — see **The Next Steps**

# Z

...is for Zzzzz.... or sleep.

If one or both of a couple has other lovers, the question of who sleeps where is always going to be an issue.

Open Fidelity is easier if each person has their own bedroom, so that they can entertain lovers without depriving their partner of somewhere to sleep.

If it feels too close for comfort for you to be in the same house as your partner and their lover, other arrangements will need to be made – perhaps including the classic choice, the hotel room, but without the classic secrecy.

Sometimes there might be three of you in a relationship, whether temporarily or long-term. When you want to sleep, will you all fit in one bed? If so, who gets the cosy (but hot) position in the middle? If not, do two people get to sleep together without the third? What if one of you snores?

The most important thing is to take everyone's needs into account and work out a solution that everyone can live with. There are no standard answers to these questions.

Z is also for Zealot – **see G for God**

# The Next Steps

Maybe you already practise polyamory or swinging, or you have an open relationship. If so, you could use this book for reference and keep a look out for more in the series. And why not give a copy to a friend or relative to help them understand your lifestyle better?

Maybe you are thinking of trying out Open Fidelity yourself. If so, this book is a good starting point. You could also look at the website (see below) to get more help and to meet others doing the same.

Or you might only just have found out about honest non-monogamy. If so, I hope you now have an impression of what Open Fidelity is all about. If you have more questions about how it works, have a look at my website, look out for future books or contact me.

Are you interested in helping the Open Fidelity project? Get in touch! You can help by:

- Spreading the word: telling all your friends to look at my website and buy this book;
- Contributing your experience: either in writing or with a recorded interview (it can be anonymous);
- Giving your expertise: on relationships and society, or on publishing, websites, marketing, publicity and the media;
- Reading my blog and commenting;
- Signing up to my email list to hear about new developments.

Website: http://www.openfidelity.info
Blog: http://ofiwriter.livejournal.com
Email: anna@openfidelity.info

# Forthcoming books on Open Fidelity

This is only the first of a series of books on Open Fidelity by Anna Sharman. Forthcoming titles are provisionally expected to include:

## Open Fidelity and Bisexuality

## Open Fidelity: a Quaker Perspective

## Open Fidelity: the Complete Guide

*Open Fidelity - an A-Z Guide* is also available in PDF format from the website (see previous page).

The website also has:

- News of the Open Fidelity project
- Details of how to access the blog, join the Open Fidelity announcements email list, or otherwise get involved with the project
- Links to related information elsewhere
- Announcements of new titles in the series
- And more!